ACTIVE Charts

Taking Anchor Charts from "Read Me" to "Try Me"

K-5

Reading ELA

Math

Science

Social Studies

Veronica Lopez

ACTIVE Anchor Charts

Taking Anchor Charts from "Read Me" to "Try Me"

K-5   Reading ELA   Math   Science   Social Studies

Veronica Lopez

ACTIVE ANCHOR CHARTS
Taking Anchor Charts from "Read Me" to "Try Me"

Veronica Lopez

Tree Top Secret Education
www.treetopsecret.com

ACTIVE ANCHOR CHARTS
Taking Anchor Charts from "Read Me" to "Try Me"

ACTIVE ANCHOR CHARTS is a trademark of Tree Top Secret,
1327 E. Washington #327 Harlingen, TX 78550

Printed in the United States of America

Special thanks to Guillermo Lopez,
the best partner a teacher and wife could ever have.

TABLE OF CONTENTS

WHAT IS AN *ACTIVE* ANCHOR CHART?

Most anchor charts are static… this means the information on the chart cannot be moved or changed. These charts provide useful content, but they only allow your students to read the information.

Active Anchor Charts are educational displays with information and materials which can be moved, sorted, heard, touched, and organized…

They take students from *"Read Me" to "Try Me."*

> "Read Me"
> to
> "Try Me."

Using the Senses

They excite the mind, eyes, ears, and fingertips.

They serve as activity boards, references, and teaching and testing tools. The pieces on the boards bring the big ideas to your students in an engaging way.

You can even add sound by attaching information and materials with hook and loop tape. The "crunching" sound and movement of pieces stimulates the brain and engages your students.

Use Active Anchor Charts for direct teaching in whole or small groups, partnered work, group work, one-to-one instruction, or independent practice, review, and testing.

When they are not in use, they serve as dynamic visual displays for each concept in Reading, Writing, Math, Science, and Social Studies. This is essential to keeping concepts front and center throughout the school year, because we all know…

If it's out of sight, it's out of mind.

> **If it's out of sight, it's out of mind.**
>
> **Let's work on changing this to…**
>
> **"In Sight & In Mind"**

BENEFITS OF *ACTIVE* ANCHOR CHARTS

A pedagogical tool is used to teach or learn a concept. Many pedagogical tools have limited uses. For example, flashcards are great but they only teach an isolated skill. You want to utilize versatile pedagogical tools that can be used with multiple instructional strategies and provide different opportunities for you to assess learning.

Meet the Active Anchor Chart Chameleon

The Active Anchor Chart Chameleon displays many of the instructional strategies you can use when you use active anchors. It also lists the various assessments that will allow you to evaluate progress.

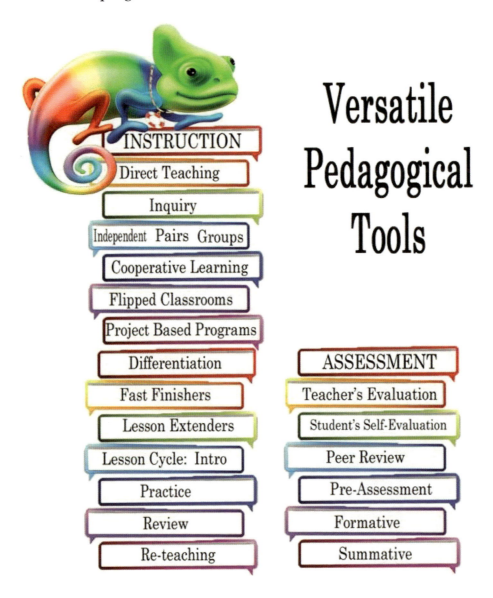

Versatile Pedagogical Tools

INSTRUCTION
Direct Teaching
Inquiry
Independent Pairs Groups
Cooperative Learning
Flipped Classrooms
Project Based Programs
Differentiation
Fast Finishers
Lesson Extenders
Lesson Cycle: Intro
Practice
Review
Re-teaching

ASSESSMENT
Teacher's Evaluation
Student's Self-Evaluation
Peer Review
Pre-Assessment
Formative
Summative

Best Teaching Practices

One Active Anchor Chart delivers information using 10 of the most effective teaching strategies:

- Your students work with a goal in mind, because the chart shows the learning target

- Display vocabulary and essential information about a concept

- Connect concepts to real-world examples

- Provide visuals and manipulatives

- Allow students to work together to discover information

- Facilitate the use of note-taking

- Give students opportunities to ask and discuss questions

- Allow students to work on problem solving

- Provide opportunities for students to practice

- Teachers and students work together to assess and recognize progress

Research has shown these strategies to be the most effective for helping students learn (Marzano, Pickering, & Pollock, 2001). Your students engage with the content and are motivated to work, ask questions, practice, learn, and show what they know.

Anchoring You as a Teacher

In the preceding section we covered ten powerful benefits of active anchor charts. Those benefits are primarily student-centered. Active anchor charts also provide many benefits that are teacher-centered. They'll help you save time and energy when you use them to prepare your lessons, teach, review, grade, assess, decorate, and organize.

They'll also... Anchor You.

- The active anchor chart serves as a lesson planning tool. It displays the learning objective, vocabulary, concepts, and activities. You'll be able to differentiate, choose modifications, assign tasks for fast finishers, and choose lesson extensions. You'll also be able to plan spiraling activities where information and skills that you have previously covered are brought around again in a current lesson. Simply pull the chart out and use it as a guide when designing lessons.

- You can use the charts during direct teaching. Display a chart as you introduce or review an objective. It will keep you focused on the main ideas. You won't forget important vocabulary and key ideas. You'll be able to demonstrate processes and show your thinking as you discuss the elements on the chart.

- Use the charts to prompt your line of questioning. The text, images, and manipulatives serve as building blocks that will help you formulate simple and complex questions. You'll demonstrate lower order and higher order thinking as you reference the context on the active anchor chart. That one context will help you introduce other contexts to help students develop L.O.T. and H.O.T.

- The charts make it easy for you to use various instructional strategies. It will take no time at all for you to decide if a chart should be used...
    - to direct teach, as practice, to review, or to assess learning.
    - by individual students, with partners, or in groups.
    - as a stand-alone activity or with other boards across several stations.
    - to introduce an idea or extend learning.

- The charts make it easier for you to evaluate a student's understanding and progress. You're able to stand back and watch students work. You can interject to check for understanding or help students move from lower order thinking to higher order thinking.

- Grading is a cinch when you use active anchor charts. Place your grade-book or a copy of your grade-book on a clipboard and walk from student to student or group to group. Pre-determine the important questions or decide on the process your students need to know in order to score an A, B, C, or failing grade.

- You can easily and quickly address misconceptions and provide effective feedback. Effective feedback helps motivate your students. This in turn helps with classroom management.

- Classroom decorating is a snap when you display your active anchor charts. You won't have to worry about updating your bulletin boards or decorations every year. The boards themselves help liven up and beautify a classroom. If you have restrictions about what you can hang up or how many items you can hang on your walls, then simply use an easel to display your charts. Another easy option is to have your students hang the boards during use. They can take them down as soon as they're done. Place your foam board active anchor charts in a large plastic box. They'll be easy to see, retrieve, replace, and store.

- Classroom organization is easier with your active anchor charts. There's less clutter and paperwork to worry about. Attach a plastic bag, pocket folder, manila folder (with taped sides), or a large envelope to your active anchor charts. Use these to store additional pieces, worksheets, supplementary information, and manipulatives.

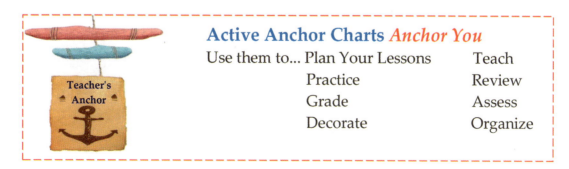

Active Anchor Charts *Anchor You*

Use them to... Plan Your Lessons   Teach

Practice   Review

Grade   Assess

Decorate   Organize

Teacher's Anchor

Picture Superiority Effect

Making Connections

Pictures are an important part of Active Anchor Charts. Images help students with recognition and recall. The picture superiority effect explains how unique pictures create a special memory trace that helps students remember the information associated with the picture (Hockley, 2008). Using several pictures for a concept helps students build connections, patterns, and contextual frameworks (Hockley, 2008; Thompson & Paivio, 1994).

Engaging With the Senses

Your students create memories as they work with the information and materials on the Active Anchor Charts. They create deeper and more memory traces when they utilize several senses (Buzan & Buzan, 1996).

The Active Anchor Charts provide opportunities for students to see, touch, move, and hear the information and materials. You can even get creative and add the sense of smell to the Active Anchor. When a smell relates to a story element, key word, or concept consider attaching a scratch and sniff sticker or misting a scented spray on the title cards and manipulatives.

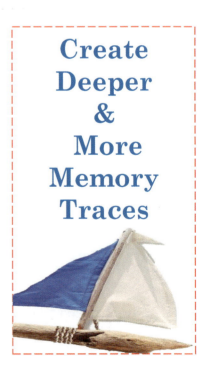

Create Deeper & More Memory Traces

TYPES OF ANCHOR CHARTS

Anchor charts serve many purposes and can be organized into three broad categories: Procedural, Informational, and Educational or P. I. E.

Procedural Charts

Procedural Charts provide students with steps to follow or the outline of a process.

Procedural Charts include but are not limited to:

- Directions
- How Tos
- Strategies
- Classroom Procedures, Campus Procedures, and Field Trip Procedures

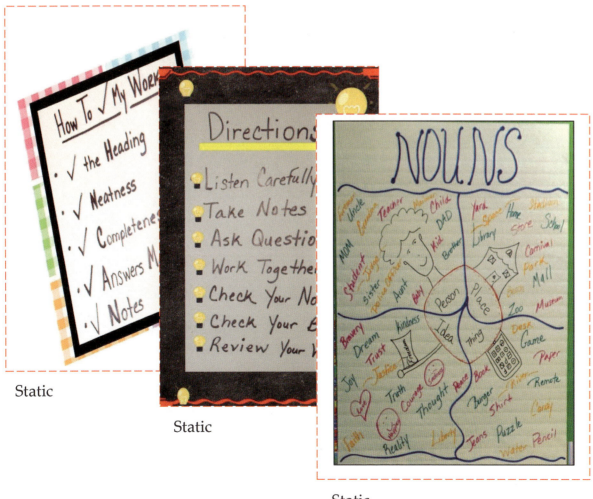

Static

Static

Static

Informational Charts

While all anchor charts provide information, Informational Charts are primarily designed to deliver knowledge. They do not ask your students to follow steps like what is required from a Procedural Chart. They do not suggest actions or provide activities like Active Anchor Charts.

Informational Charts include but are not limited to:

- Rules - Classroom and Discipline
- Signs
- Schedules
- Quotes - Inspirational and Motivational
- Theory (for use by teachers or students)

Static

Static

Static

Educational Charts

Educational charts deliver instructional content. They provide information and materials related to Reading, ELA/Writing, Mathematics, Science, Social Studies, and all other content areas. They can also target cross-disciplinary studies. Educational Charts are the most effective when they are created as Active Anchor Charts.

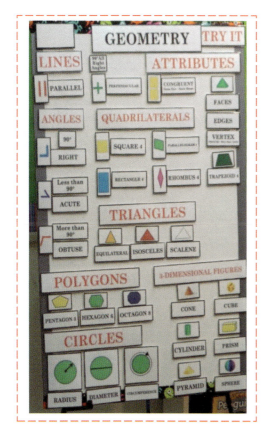

Active

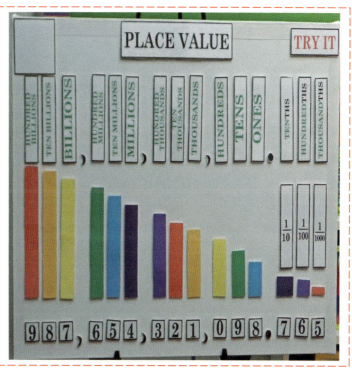

Active

Static Anchor Charts and Active Anchor Charts

All three of these charts can be static… information does not move or change.

All three of these charts can be made into Active Anchor Charts… information and materials move or change.

Since your energy, time, and funds are limited, you may want to limit your focus to Educational Charts. Educational charts are best delivered as Active Anchor Charts, because they help your students learn and practice concepts by moving and changing information and materials.

P. I. E. Anchor Charts

Anchor Chart Types are as easy as... **P**rocedural, **I**nformational, and **E**ducational

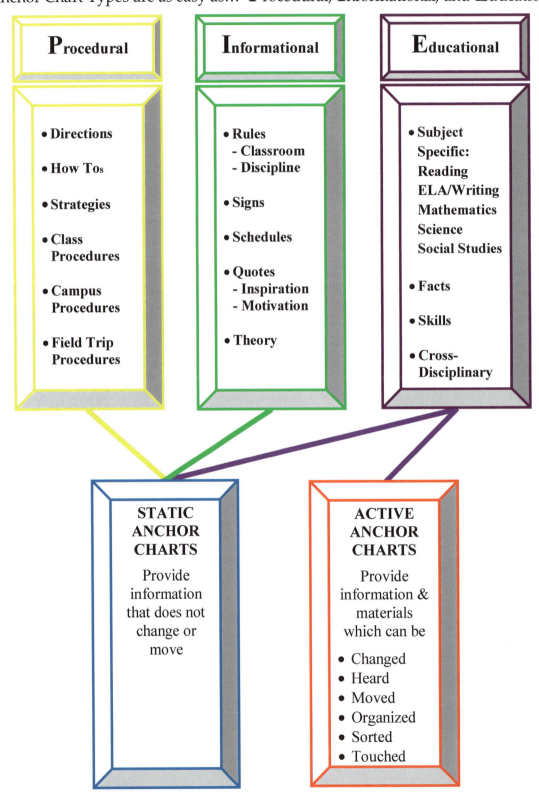

Procedural

- Directions
- How Tos
- Strategies
- Class Procedures
- Campus Procedures
- Field Trip Procedures

Informational

- Rules
  - Classroom
  - Discipline
- Signs
- Schedules
- Quotes
  - Inspiration
  - Motivation
- Theory

Educational

- Subject Specific: Reading ELA/Writing Mathematics Science Social Studies
- Facts
- Skills
- Cross-Disciplinary

STATIC ANCHOR CHARTS

Provide information that does not change or move

ACTIVE ANCHOR CHARTS

Provide information & materials which can be

- Changed
- Heard
- Moved
- Organized
- Sorted
- Touched

CREATING YOUR *ACTIVE* ANCHOR CHARTS

7 Steps for Creating Your *Active* Anchor Chart

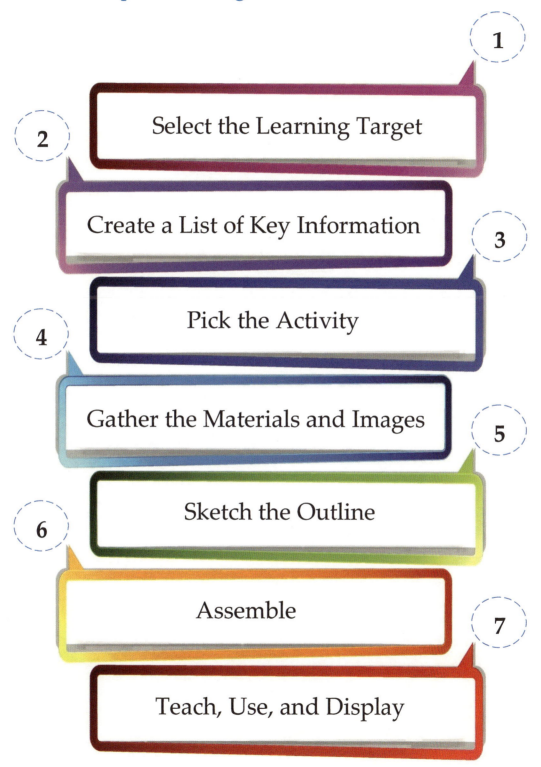

1. Select the Learning Target

2. Create a List of Key Information

3. Pick the Activity

4. Gather the Materials and Images

5. Sketch the Outline

6. Assemble

7. Teach, Use, and Display

Creating Your *Active* Anchor Chart

Follow these steps to create your active anchor chart…

1 - Select the learning target, standard, concept, strategy, process, or skill.

2 - Create a list of the vocabulary terms, process steps, information, and images associated with this learning target.

3 - Decide on an activity that will allow your students to work with the information on the anchor chart. The information, images, questions, and problems can be…

- Compared
- Drawn
- Graphed
- Identified
- Labeled
- Listed
- Matched
- Memorized
- Moved
- Named
- Ordered
- Organized
- Recited
- Removed
- Solved
- Sorted
- Switched
- Translated

4 - Gather the materials and images you will need to create your active anchor chart. This includes the board or paper for the chart itself, drawing tools, and display materials. You will need to create cards for your titles, subtitles, text, and some images.

5 - Sketch an outline of your chart. Draw exactly where the information, images, and manipulatives will be placed.

6 - Assemble the active anchor chart. Decide if you want to do this with your students or in advance of the lesson. If you want your students to have a say in the labels and images to include, then have some blank cards available. Use hook and loop tape to attach a small or gallon size re-sealable bag to the back of your anchor chart. Materials should be placed inside the bag when they are not in use.

7 - Your Active Anchor Chart is ready. Use it to teach and reinforce the learning target. Have your students complete the Active Anchor Chart activity. They can work with a partner, in groups, or independently. Display the chart in an easy to reach and easy to see location.

See the Active Anchor Chart ESSENTIALS on the next page…

Target:
- Standard
- Learning
  Objective
- Date

TITLE
Bold, Clear, and Simple

Call to Action:
- Try Me
- Pick Me Up
- Let's Work

SUBTITLES
Use VISUALS and TEXT for
CONCEPTS and CONTEXT

Add COLOR

Leave

White

Space

Be ORGANIZED

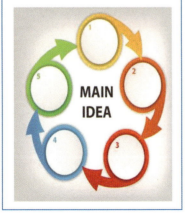

MAIN IDEA

Include an ACTIVITY

- Compared
- Drawn
- Graphed
- Identified
- Labeled
- Listed
- Matched
- Memorized
- Moved

- Named
- Ordered
- Organized
- Recited
- Removed
- Solved
- Sorted
- Switched
- Translated

Attach MANIPULATIVES

ACTIVE ANCHOR CHART LEARNING TARGETS and SAMPLE ACTIVE ANCHOR BOARDS

READING

Alphabet
Antonyms
Author's Purpose
Authors
Autobiographies
Biographies
Blends
Cause and Effect
Character Analysis
Character Traits
Compare and Contrast
Consonants
Context Clues
Credits
Dictionary
Dolch Words
Draw Conclusions
Entertain
Evidence
Fact and Opinions
Fairy Tales
Fantasy
Fiction
Finding the Right Book
Flashbacks
Folktales
Genre
Glossaries
Graphic Organizers
Graphs

Idioms
Illustrators
Inferences
Inform
Labels
Language – Literal &
Figurative
Long and Short Sounds
Lower and Upper Case
Letters
Main Idea
Mental Imagery
Menus
Multiple Meaning
Words
Mysteries
Myths
Nonfiction
Novels
Paraphrase
Parts of a Book
Persuade
Phonemes
Plot
Poetry
Point of View
Predictions
Prefixes and Suffixes
Pronunciation
Prose

Proverbs
References
Rereading
Retelling
Root Words
Sequence
Setting
Sight Words
Story Elements
Summarize
Supporting Details
Syllables
Synonyms
Synthesize
Table of Contents
Tall Tales
Text Features
Themes
Tone and Mood
Transitions
Vocabulary
Vowels
What Good Readers Do
What We Read
Who, What, When,
Where, Why, & How
Why We Read
Word Blends

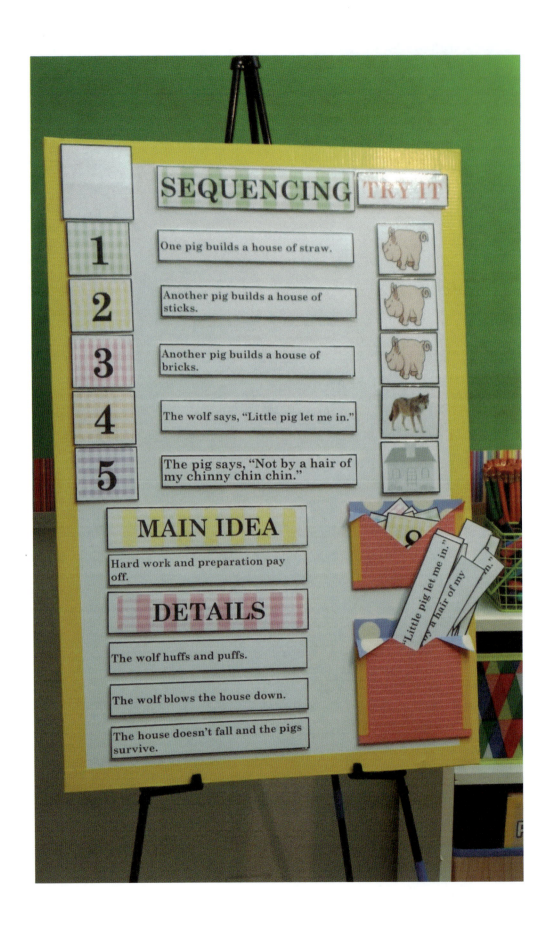

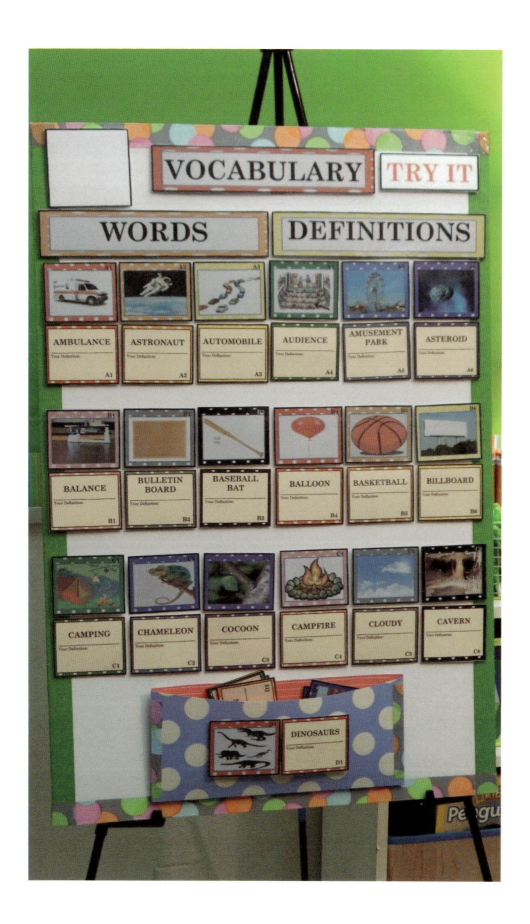

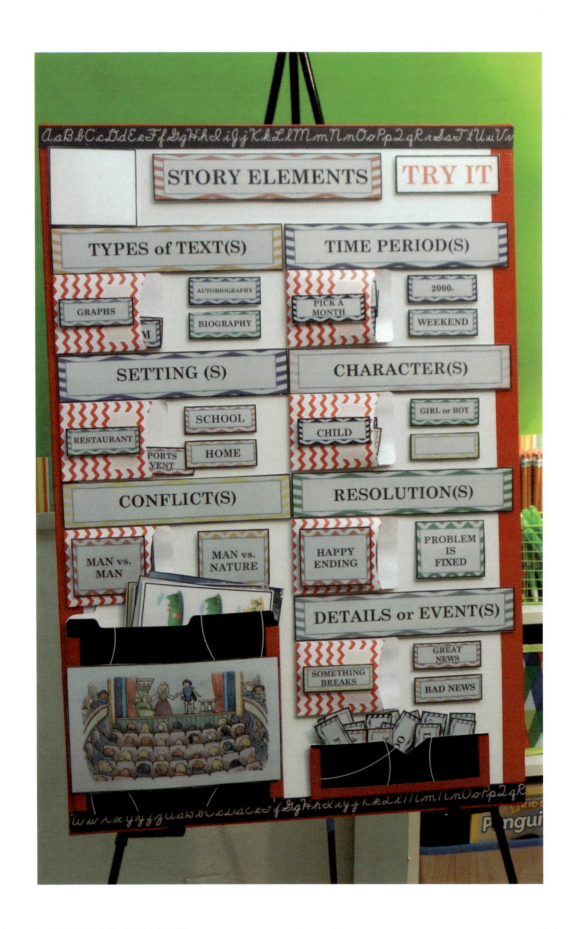

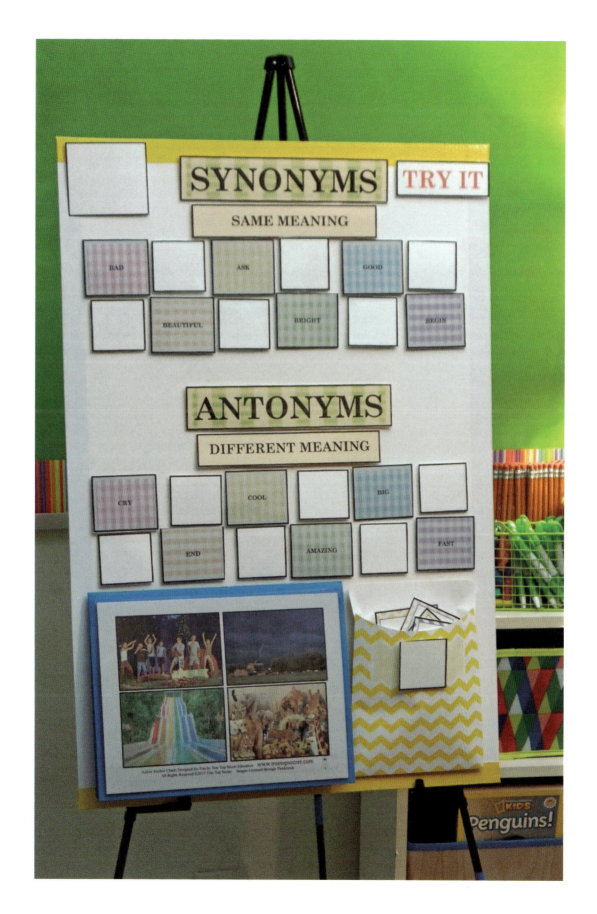

Adjectives
Adverbs
Articles
Capitalization
Comma Splices
Commas
Common Writing Mistakes
Complex Sentences
Compound Sentences
Conjunctions
Contractions
Declarative Sentences
Dependent Clauses
Dictionaries
Drafts
Essays
Expository Writing
Final Draft
Formal and Informal Language
Frequently Confused Words
Frequently Misspelled Words
Indenting
Independent Clauses
Interjections
Interrogative Sentences
Narrative Writing
Nouns
Paragraphs
Parallel Structure
Parts of an Essay
Periods

Persuasive Writing
Point of View
Possessives
Predicates
Prefixes
Prepositions
Pre-writing
Prompts
Pronouns
Proofreading
Proper Nouns
Punctuation
Quotations
Root Words
Run-On Sentences
Sentence Construction
Sentence Fragments
Simple Sentences
Singular and Plural
Spelling
Subjects
Subject-Verb and Pronoun-Antecedent
     Agreement
Suffixes
Syllable Patterns
Verb Tenses
Verbs
Vocabulary
Voice
Word Choice
Word Families

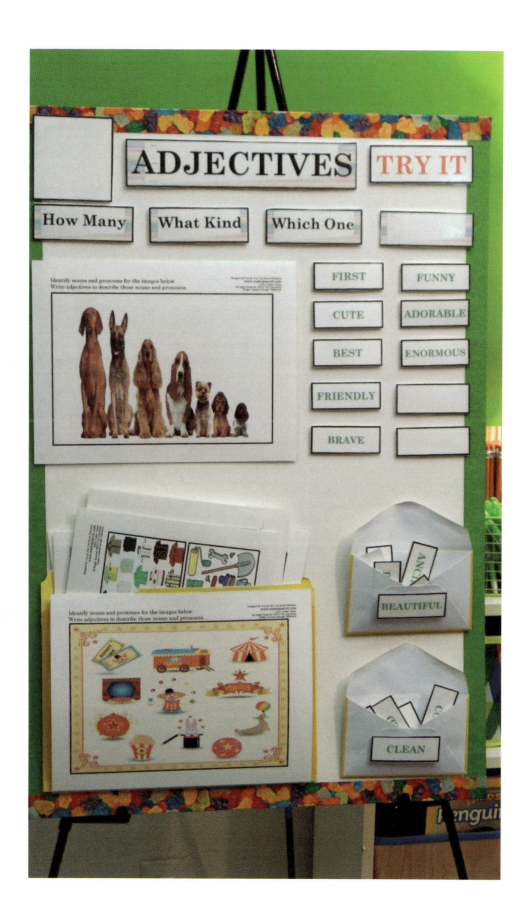

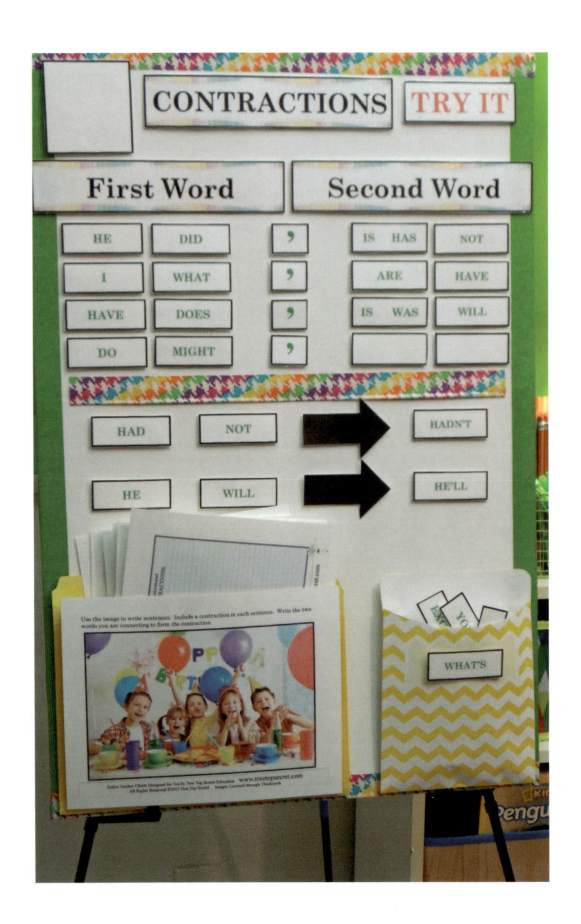

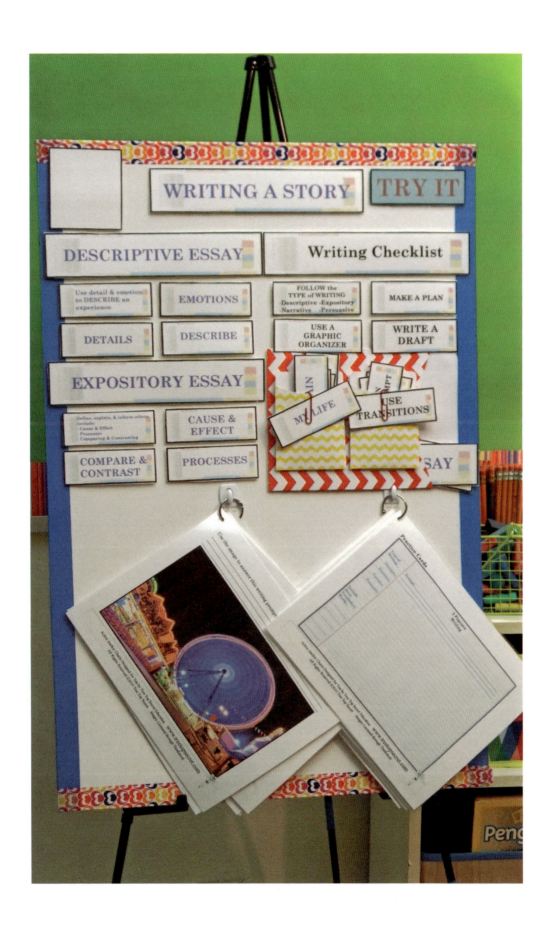

MATHEMATICS

2-Dimensional Shapes
3-Dimensional Objects
Addition
Angles
Area
Arrays
Attributes
Balances
Bar Graphs
Budgets
Calculators
Cardinal Numbers
Circle Graphs
Clocks
Comparing Numbers
Composite Numbers
Congruency
Conversions
Coordinate Grid
Counting
Decimals
Division
Equations
Equivalent Fractions
Factors
Finances
Fractions

Geometry
Greater Than and Less
Than
Guess and Check
Height
Improper Fractions
Learn My Numbers
Length
Line Graphs
Lines
Mathematicians
Measurement
Mixed Numbers
Money
Multiples
Multiplication
Multiplication of 10s
and 100s
Number Sentences
Numerators &
Denominators
Odd and Even Numbers
Order of Operations
Ordered Pairs
Ordering Numbers
Parts to Wholes
Patterns

Perimeter
Pictographs
Place Value
Prime Numbers
Probability
Problem Solving
Purchasing
Ratios
Rulers
Saving
Scatter Plots
Sequencing
Skip Counting
Sorting
Spending
Subtraction
Symmetry
Temperatures
Thermometers
Time
Tools
Transformations
Vocabulary
Volume
Whole Numbers
Width
Work Backwards

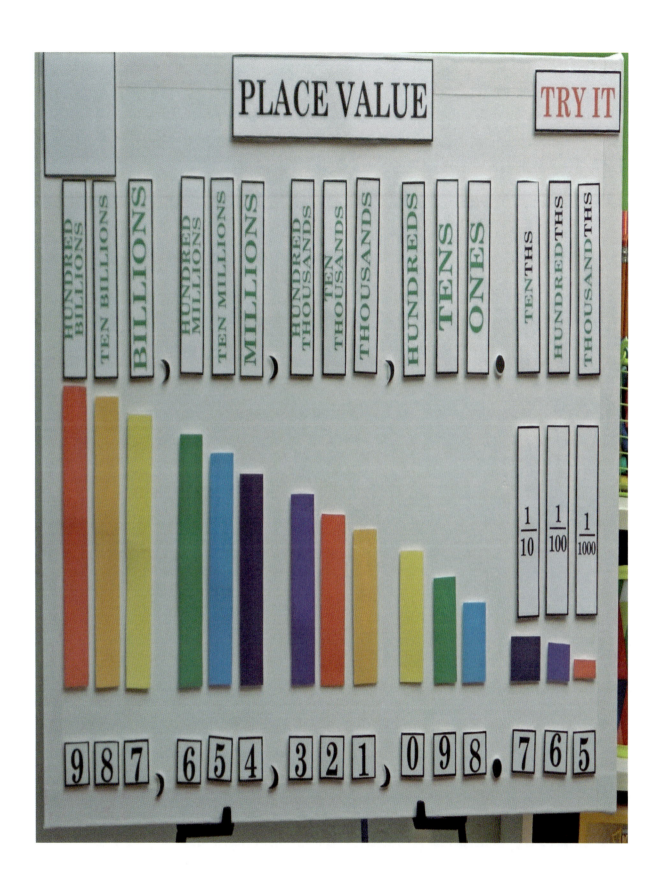

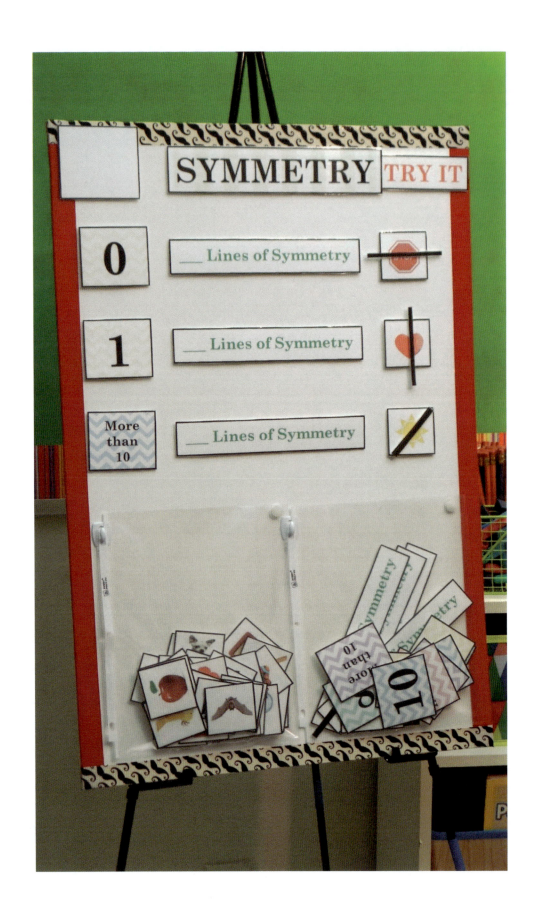

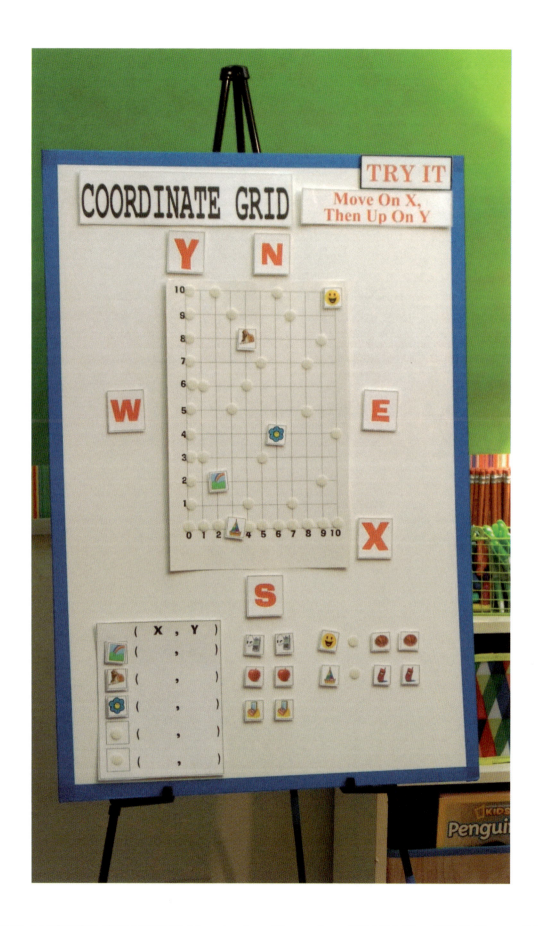

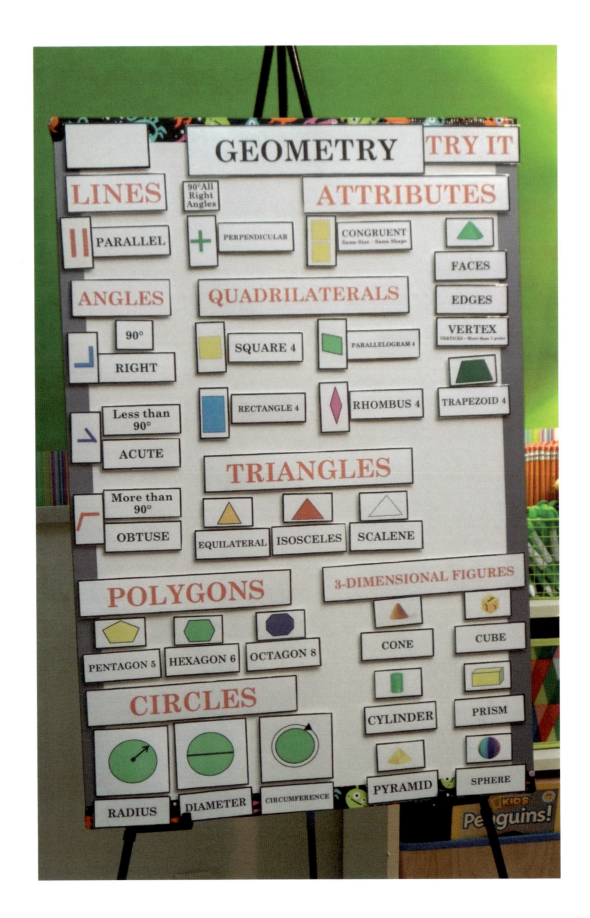

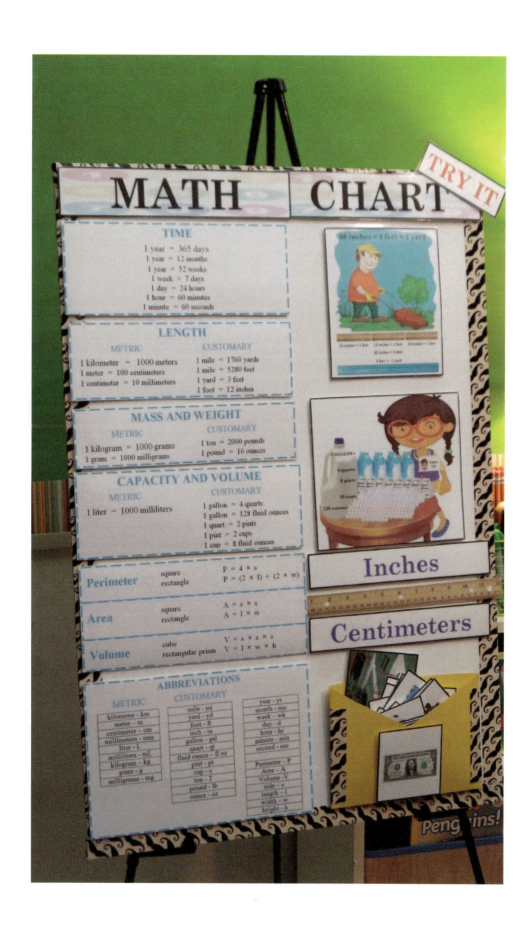

MATH CHART

TRY IT

TIME

1 year = 365 days
1 year = 12 months
1 year = 52 weeks
1 week = 7 days
1 day = 24 hours
1 hour = 60 minutes
1 minute = 60 seconds

LENGTH

METRIC	CUSTOMARY
1 kilometer = 1000 meters	1 mile = 1760 yards
1 meter = 100 centimeters	1 mile = 5280 feet
1 centimeter = 10 millimeters	1 yard = 3 feet
	1 foot = 12 inches

MASS AND WEIGHT

METRIC	CUSTOMARY
1 kilogram = 1000 grams	1 ton = 2000 pounds
1 gram = 1000 milligrams	1 pound = 16 ounces

CAPACITY AND VOLUME

METRIC	CUSTOMARY
1 liter = 1000 milliliters	1 gallon = 4 quarts
	1 gallon = 128 fluid ounces
	1 quart = 2 pints
	1 pint = 2 cups
	1 cup = 8 fluid ounces

Perimeter	square	$P = 4 \times s$
	rectangle	$P = (2 \times l) + (2 \times w)$
Area	square	$A = s \times s$
	rectangle	$A = l \times w$
Volume	cube	$V = s \times s \times s$
	rectangular prism	$V = l \times w \times h$

ABBREVIATIONS

METRIC	CUSTOMARY	
kilometer - km	mile - mi	year - yr
meter - m	yard - yd	month - mo
centimeter - cm	foot - ft	week - wk
millimeters - mm	inch - in	day - d
liter - L	gallon - gal	hour - hr
milliliters - mL	quart - qt	minute - min
kilogram - kg	fluid ounce - fl oz	second - sec
gram - g	pint - pt	
milligrams - mg	cup - c	Perimeter - P
	ton - T	Area - A
	pound - lb	Volume - V
	ounce - oz	side - s
		length - l
		width - w
		height - h

Inches

Centimeters

SCIENCE

Adaptations
Alternative Energy Sources
Animal Cells
Animal Kingdom
Atoms
Body Systems
Buoyancy
Carbon Cycle
Climate
Compounds
Conservation
Density
Deposition
Discoveries
Earth
Earth Science
Earthquakes
Electricity
Elements
Endangered Species
Energy
Erosion
Ethics
Exercise
Food Chains
Food Webs
Fossil Fuels
Fossils
Friction

Galaxy
Gravity
Habitats
Health
Hurricanes
Inertia
Inherited and Learned Traits
Inventions
Landforms
Layers of the Earth
Life Cycle
Life Science
Light
Mass
Matter
Measuring
Minerals
Mixtures
Moon
Natural Disasters
Nature of Science
Niches
Nitrogen Cycle
Period Table of Elements
Physical Science
Plant Cells
Plant Kingdom
Recycling

Resources
Revolving
Rock Cycle
Rocks
Rotation
Safety Rules
Scientific Method
Scientists
Seasons
Simple Machines
Six Kingdoms of Life
Soil
Solar System
Solutions
Sound
States of Matter
Sun
Tides
Tools
Tornadoes
Universe
Vertebrates and Invertebrates
Vocabulary
Volume
Water Cycle
Waves
Weather
Weathering
Weight

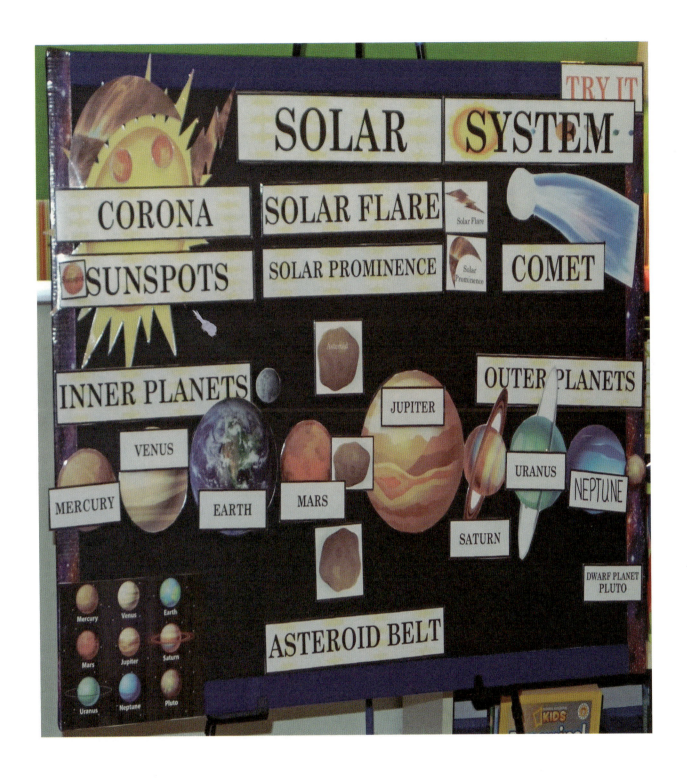

SOCIAL STUDIES

Agriculture

American Revolution

Ancient Civilizations

Archaeology

Articles of
Confederation

Aztec Empire

Biographies

Boston Tea Party

Branches of Government

British Colonies

Capitals

Cities

Civics

Civil Rights Movement

Civil War

Climate

Cold War

Colonial Times

Congress

Continents

Countries

Cuban-Missile Crisis

Cultures

Current Events

Declaration of
Independence

Discoveries

Early Man

Economics

Equality

European Explorers

Exploration

Flags

French and Indian War

Geography

Governments

Great Depression

Historians

Holidays

Holocaust

Immigration

Industrial Revolution

Internet

Inventions

Kings

Labor Movement

Landforms

Languages

Laws

Legislature

Local News

Maps

Mayan Empire

Media

Mexican War

Monuments

Native Americans

Neighborhoods

Oceans

Political Maps

Politics

Presidents

Queens

Reconstruction

Religions

Renaissance Period

Roman Empire

Royalty

Slavery

Space Race

Spanish-American War

States

Symbols

Technology

The Louisiana Purchase

The Monroe Doctrine

The War of 1812

Time Periods

Timelines

Topography

Traditions

Transportation

United Nations

United States

United States
Constitution

Victorian Era

Vietnam War

Voting Rights

Westward Expansion

World War I

World War II

MATERIALS

Options for Backgrounds/Canvases

Active Anchors can be created on a variety of materials. You'll want to consider where the charts will be displayed, your budget, and supplies you may already have on hand.

Backgrounds:	Price Range:
Butcher Paper	No Cost: Check school workroom White: $10 and up/Roll Color: $15 and up/Roll
Chart Paper	$24/Pad of 25 Sheets
Commercial Posters	No Cost: Recycle your posters $1 and up
Fabric	$1 and up/Yard
File Folders	$8 -$10/Box of 100
Foam Boards	White: $1 Black or Color: $2 to $4
Paper Bags	Free: Recycle your paper bags $2 to $3 for a bag of 50 or more
PlexiGlass	$5 and up depending on size
Poster Board	White: $1 or less Color: $2
Scrapbook Paper	$1 and up/Sheet
Sketch Pads	$5 and up/Pad of 25
SmartFab	$1 and up/Yard
Wrapping Paper	$1 to $5/Roll

Butcher Paper

Your school's workroom is probably equipped with a few colors of butcher paper. We have to consider it as an option, because the paper is huge and FREE. You will have to cut the paper down into a size which fits the laminating machine, but at such a great price you can't pass it up. Once the paper is laminated it offers a great colorful surface for hook and loop tape, sticky notes, and tape. Your local teacher supply store may carry printed butcher paper. Prints include clouds, jungle, wood, grass, and others.

Chart Paper

Chart paper is the traditional medium for creating anchor charts. Lined chart paper is great for keeping text straight and organized. Some chart papers have an adhesive backing, but the stickiness wears off after you move the paper a few times. Save your money and choose the more affordable non-adhesive paper. You can always use tape, hooks, push pins, or hook and loop tape to display your chart.

If you are creating a teacher-made chart, then you can laminate the paper before use. The laminate will keep the paper from tearing. This is especially important if your students will be using the charts on a regular basis. You are likely creating charts that will be useful year after year, and the laminate will protect them while they are on display, are in use, or are stored.

Chart paper tablets are available in various sizes and colors.

Commercial Posters

It always feels great when you can recycle some old things instead of spending even more of your hard earned money on classroom supplies. Look at your collection of commercial posters and up-cycle them into anchor charts. The backs of many of these posters are left blank and will make excellent blank canvases for your anchor charts. These posters have an added benefit if they are already laminated. The laminate will allow you to easily attach and detach hook and loop tape. If you no longer use a poster but it has some large text and amazing images, then by all means cut them out and use them as pieces for your customized anchor charts.

Fabric

You may not find a more versatile material than fabric. There are countless colors, patterns, textiles, and sizes to choose from. Prices vary and some discount bins may include a yard of fabric for less than a buck. While you can use the fabric as is, you will have to stop fraying by binding it with a sewing machine, glue, or tape. You can always save the trouble and laminate the fabric. As with some of the other options, you should find colors and patterns which relate to the topics of your anchor charts. A jungle print would be great for habitats in science. A thin lined print would be fantastic for mathematical anchor charts which focus on coordinate grids, graphs, or number lines. A wider lined fabric would work nicely for writing anchor charts.

File Folders, a.k.a. Manila Folders

File folders or manila folders are available in a variety of colors. Whether you use the letter size or legal size versions, you will find they provide a sturdy canvas area for your anchor charts. These are cheap, compact, and easy to store… you can create a classroom set or have students create individual charts for personal use.

Foam Boards

Many of us have used foam boards for science fair projects, craft projects, and various presentations. They are sturdy, durable, inexpensive, and lightweight. They also come in a variety of sizes, colors, and thicknesses. A large, 20" by 30", white foam board will cost a buck at your local dollar store. Not all dollar stores carry color or black foam boards, but you can find them in local discount stores, craft and hobby shops, school supply stores, office supply stores, and online retailers. The color and black foam boards cost a little more, so be on the look-out for sales or coupons.

Paper Bags

Here you have another recycling/up-cycling opportunity. You can choose to design your anchor chart on the bag then laminate or laminate the bag first and then add the

elements of your active anchor chart. You can unglue the bag, cut it to create straight edges, and laminate. However, you can also laminate a closed bag. Use a pair of scissors to cut the bag open and you'll have a well to bring your active anchor charts up to the "BLOWING MY MIND" level. You can design the anchor chart on the exterior of the bag, and use the well of the bag to hold related manipulatives, models, maps, books, notes, and student samples.

Plexiglass

Stick with me on this one... I know plexiglass sounds expensive but the durability and flexibility of this plastic makes it a great option for anchor charts. The truth is... plexiglass has a COOL factor which makes it hard to pass up. Think of those movies where you see professional creative types or geeky IT teams designing their master plans on clear glass panes. While safety concerns and budgets keep us from that level of coolness, we can still create that same vibe with plexiglass. You can purchase a plexiglass sheet at your local home-improvement store.

Poster Boards

Posters boards aren't just for art and science projects anymore. Posters boards are a wonderful choice, because they are sturdy, cheap, and available in a variety of colors. Prices range from fifty cents to $2. You may even have a few on hand if your school includes them on the school supplies list. Some school administrators allot a small budget ($100 or a little more) to each teacher at the start and end of the school year. If you are fortunate enough to get this allotment, then consider placing an order for a larger quantity of posters. You could even combine your order with those of other teachers – You'll save even more because many school supplies vendors offer a deeper discount on larger quantity purchases.

Scrapbook Paper

12" by 12" scrapbook paper sheets are available for $1 or less. They come in solid colors and a variety of patterns. Once laminated the paper makes for a durable surface on which you can adhere your active anchor chart pieces. Scrapbook paper pads are available in a variety of themes. These will come in handy if you are working a thematic unit. You can use coordinating papers to create sets of related anchor charts and use them in learning stations.

Sketch Pads

Sketch Pads, also called artist pads, are available in a variety of sizes. The paper comes in various thicknesses and colors. These pads cost a little more, but each pad may have 25, 50, or more sheets. They are available at craft and hobby shops. Be on the look-out for weekly and seasonal sales and coupons from circulars or online stores.

Laminate the sheets then use them as canvases for your active anchor charts.

SmartFab

SmartFab® is a non-woven fabric… think of the material from those inexpensive shopping totes you find at the grocery store. SmartFab® is available at teacher supply stores and online. It is stable and more durable than paper. It comes in a range of vibrant colors and can be laminated. Some teacher supply stores carry large rolls, similar to large butcher paper rolls, and you can certainly create a huge anchor chart from a large sheet. However, you'll need to consider the size of the laminating machine if you plan on laminating your SmartFab®. Stock up on SmartFab when your local teacher supply store has back to school or holiday specials and discounts.

Wrapping Paper

Wrapping paper designs and thicknesses have come a long way. You can find a variety of colors, patterns, and types at dollar stores, department stores, gift shops, and craft stores. Prices vary but you can usually pick up a roll for a dollar or two. Consider a print which corresponds to the topic of your anchor chart. Imagine an adaptations (science) anchor chart set against a lizard print wrapping paper. How about a lines and angles anchor chart against a geometric pattern. For reading, pick patterns which match the storylines of your books.

Options for Writing and Drawing Tools

The paintbrushes or writing and drawing tools you will use to create your anchor charts are only limited by your imagination. You can use pencils, pens, regular markers, dry erase markers, permanent markers, chalk, printers, die-cut machines and even paint.

Chalk

If you are using black paper or black foam board, then chalk will create some nice image and text effects. You may be worried the chalk will easily smudge or be erased. You can spritz the completed anchor chart with hairspray. A pricier option is using a Fixative spray. Fixative sprays are especially made for sealing chalk and other mediums. Fixatives can be found at craft and hobby stores, art supply stores, and online.

Craft Foam Shapes

Craft foam is sold in solid sheets, but is also sold in cut-outs of letters, animals, geometric figures, and many other shapes. These shapes add a 3-dimensional quality to your anchor chart. The foam is available in various sizes, thicknesses, and colors. Some foam is designed with glitter or patterns. Some of the foam shapes are backed with adhesive and can  be easily attached to your anchor chart. The non-adhesive shapes can be glued onto the chart. You can find these shapes in craft stores and discount department stores.

Die-cut Machines

Die-cut machines are amazing tools. Your school may have one in the workroom or you may own a personal machine. Consider designing some of your text on the machine. You can also create some beautiful visuals for your anchor charts. The possibilities are endless, because there are thousands of die-cut images and letters available.

Markers

Many of the canvases or surfaces of your anchor charts will be laminated. This means you can use dry erase and permanent markers. Dry erase markers are an excellent choice if you will have students explaining the flow of a cycle, graphing information, or adding their own information. Don't worry about not being able to erase a mistake when using a permanent marker, because a little nail polish remover usually does the trick. If you do use the nail polish remover, make sure to use it out of the reach or smell of your students.

Crayola®, RoseArt®, and generic brand markers will work for your non-laminated materials. Be sure to check for bleed-through if you are writing on a stack of papers. Stop bleed-through by placing a piece of cardboard behind the paper.

Consider using markers with various thicknesses. Some text needs the finesse and whimsy of a thin line. Other text needs the grand and bold statement only a thicker line will convey.

Paint

Paint is not the best option for many of your anchor charts, but it shouldn't be excluded from your creative toolbox. There are many options for paint. Paints can add texture, neon, a glow-in-the-dark effect, glitter effects, or 3-D/puffy effects. You can use the paint to outline or fill in text and images.

Craft paints and foam application brushes are a great option because they are inexpensive. The paints come in many colors, dry quickly, apply easily, and most wash out nicely.

Pencils and Pens

Pencils will work in a pinch. The only real concern is to make the print as dark as possible, because a light touch will make the text difficult to read from a distance. A pencil is also great for adding shadow or emphasis to your text.

Your standard blue and black ink pens are easy and inexpensive tools for creating text and word-art. Pens are also available in a variety of colors and there are a few inexpensive brands you can pick up at your local dollar store.

Printers

Your computer's word processing program has built-in fonts and clipart. You can quickly design and print individual words, definitions, quotes, shapes, charts, and images. If you are fortunate enough to have a color printer, then color is always the way to go. However, black and white printers will work great if you use block fonts and black-line images. Just print and start coloring away. With thin markers and a box of colors, you'll create beautiful anchor chart manipulatives in no time. (Keep copyright issues in mind when using clipart.)

Stencils

Alphabet stencils are another great tool for adding a dramatic touch to your titles, categories, or graphs. Your craft and hobby shop will have a wide selection of stencils.

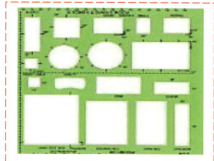

These may include geometric shapes for your math anchor charts and animal and landscape shapes for your science and social studies anchor charts. Stencil prices will vary, but you can usually find simpler stencils for a few dollars. Consider using cookie cutters as stencils, because they are inexpensive and often sold in sets. Stencils are easy to use and your students will be able to handle them with only a little instruction and guidance.

PUTTING THE *ACTIVE* IN YOUR
ACTIVE ANCHOR CHARTS

Your anchor chart moves from being a static (non-moving) display to being an active anchor chart once you add materials that can be moved. You will need to add titles, subtitles, terms, explanations, images, and manipulatives. The items and information can be…

- Compared
- Drawn
- Graphed
- Identified
- Labeled
- Listed
- Matched
- Memorized
- Moved

- Named
- Ordered
- Organized
- Recited
- Removed
- Solved
- Sorted
- Switched
- Translated

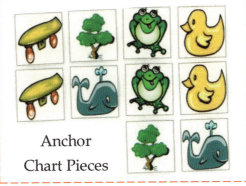

Anchor
Chart Pieces

Attaching Text, Images, and Manipulatives

There are no limits to the resources you can use to attach, display, and store the pieces of your Active Anchor Charts. Look for a variety of envelopes, plastic baggies, binder clips, binder rings, double stick hooks, hook and loop tape, paper or lunch bags, job ticket holders, sheet protectors, manila folders, library pockets, and small plastic bins. You can also recycle cardboard boxes and plastic cleaning wipe dispensers like the ones shown in the bottom left corner below.

Hook and Loop Tape

The method you use for attaching the text, images, and manipulatives will depend on the canvas you use. In most cases, the best option is hook and loop tape. Hook and loop tape is sold in rolls, squares, and circles (called coins).

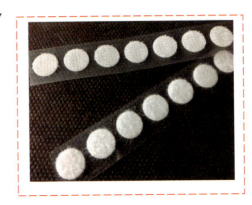

Hook and loop tape will make it easy for your students to remove and replace the pieces. Be consistent about which side will be placed on the anchor charts and which will be adhered to the pieces. For example, decide to stick all the loop (softer side) pieces to the charts and the hook (rougher side) to the pieces. This ensures that each piece can be attached on any point of the chart.

Placement of the pieces will require a plan. Once you decide on the learning target and activity for the board, you will want to sketch out a plan for the placement of all the pieces. Gather and create the necessary materials. Place all the pieces on the canvas and move them around until they are in the right order or are organized. Once the pieces are in the right places, begin placing the hook and loop tape on each piece and attach it to the canvas. The next step is to display your active anchor chart.

Repositionable Tools

Post-it notes are a great repositionable tool. They come in a variety of shapes, sizes, and colors. You can quickly add information to a post-it note, place it on the chart, and later reposition it.

Elmer's also has a repositionable glue stick that you can use to convert any piece or sheet of paper into an anchor chart tool. You just swipe the repositionable glue on the back of the paper and attach the paper to the chart.

Of course, the longevity of the glue on the paper or post-it note will depend on how often the paper is repositioned.

Converting Store Bought Posters and Static Anchor Charts

Store Bought Posters

You don't have to start from scratch when it comes to creating your active anchor charts.

We often buy store bought posters, because we need a visual tool to help us communicate information to our students. However, these posters tend to either have way too much information or not enough information. They also present technical vocabulary and processes that students aren't ready to learn.

Those words and ideas become distracters - the last thing we want to do is distract or confuse our students.

Static Anchor Charts

You also may have invested tons of time creating static anchor charts. These charts present the right vocabulary and processes, but they can only be viewed and not manipulated.

Students follow the idea as you are introducing or reviewing the information on these charts, but are lost when they have to view the chart on their own. If you created the charts with help from your students, then they probably understood the connections that were being made at the time (if they were ALL listening and on task).

> **More than**
>
> **half**
>
> **is forgotten**
>
> **by the end**
>
> **of the lesson.**
>
> **(Buzan & Buzan, 1996)**

Research tells us that more than half of the information will be forgotten by the end of the session (Buzan & Buzan, 1996). Students will not remember all the links and meanings after the creation session is over. This is probably why you have students who seem to have forgotten everything by the time they return to class the next day.

Workbooks, Flashcards, and Other Printed Materials

Search your room for items that are rarely used but are colorful and large enough to use on an active anchor chart.

Old workbooks, textbooks, children's books, and teacher's resources might be collecting dust in a cabinet or storage box. Take a look at your sets of flashcards. You may find a few that are damaged or are no longer used.

Incomplete games and activity sets are full of treasures that can add some spark to your active anchor charts. Look for other printed materials in your classroom, around your home, in the mail, at your grocery store, in the newspaper, museums, and tourist centers.

You'll be amazed at the many sources of printed materials that are available once you make it your mission to find them.

> ## Find Printed Materials at the
> ## Grocery Store, Hotel Desk, Visitor's Bureau, Museums, and Gift Shops

Converting Posters, Static Anchor Charts, and Printed Materials

Your store bought posters and static anchor charts can easily be converted into active anchor charts.

Follow these simple steps...

- Identify the charts with large text and great visuals
- Cut out the text and visuals
- Laminate the text and visuals (save time by using pre-laminated posters)
- Cut the lamination
- Attach the pieces, mix and match where you can, on a background

Voila! Your new active anchor chart takes students from "Read Me to Try Me!"

White Space

Leave plenty of white space, blank areas, around the text and materials on your board. White space is important because...

- It provides a place for the eyes to rest as they scan the information.

- It helps the text, images, and materials to visually stand out or pop-off the page.

- It is available when you need to add additional information or tips. You may even use the space to add insights from your students.

- It makes for a cleaner and visually appealing design.

Limited White Space

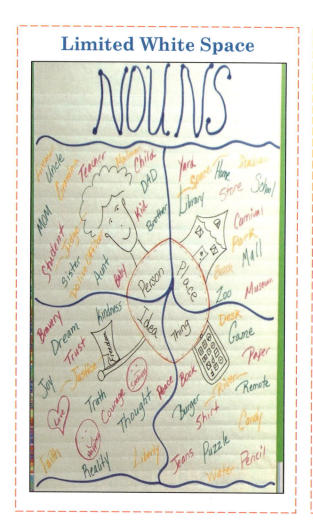

Great Use of White Space

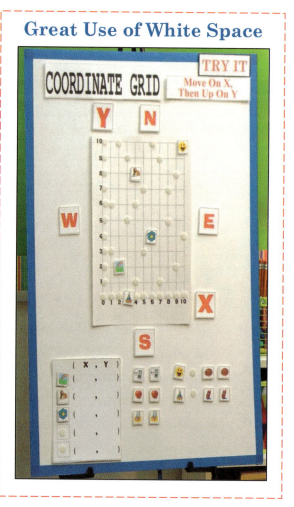

DISPLAYING YOUR MASTERPIECES

There are many ways to display your anchor charts. You can use tape, magnets, glue, push-pins, staples, string, fishing line, putty, paper clips, binder clips, hook and loop tape, easels, and hooks. Beware of using nails or screws, because you will most certainly incur the wrath of your principal. One principal explained it this way, "I am responsible for making sure the wall is still structurally sound long after we're gone." Masonry, paneling, and sheet rock take a beating after a few teachers have used the room. It makes environmental and economic sense to use a light touch when displaying our masterpieces.

Always test the adhesive in a small and out of the way space. You'll be able to make sure the adhesive works and ensure it doesn't damage the wall or surface area.

To save time and frustration, take the time to measure and mark where your anchor chart will be displayed. It can be frustrating when you realize you have to remove glue or move your tape and hooks, because the chart is crooked. Start the process by identifying where the chart will be displayed. Measure the area and the anchor chart. Use a straight edge and pencil to place a few guiding marks on the display surface.

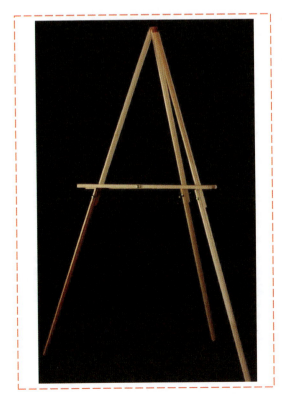

Easels

Desktop or floor easels are a special way to display your anchor charts. They are available in lightweight metal or wood. Prices start at about $10 for a desktop easel. They can be purchased at art supply stores, craft and hobby stores, office supply stores, and online. You can use a desktop easel on the floor or in a reading corner. Since floor easels take up quite a bit of space, they will not work in every classroom. You can decide to use one easel to feature an anchor chart. Easels are light enough that a student(s) can easily move it into place to display then explain an anchor chart.

Fishing Line

Fishing line can be threaded into the holes of an anchor chart. The line can easily be tied into a strong knot. This approach works best if the chart is made on a thicker material or if it is laminated. You can also tape the line directly to the anchor chart or tie it onto a clip that is holding the chart. The beauty of fishing line is it can be hung from any point on your wall or ceiling. Form a loop with the fishing line to hang it from hooks. Many classrooms have a system of rails which create a dropped ceiling. You can thread the line through or around the rails and easily adjust the display height of the anchor chart.

Glue

Low-temp and hi-temp glue guns will work if you are not planning on moving the anchor chart. Always test the glue in a small area, because some brands will cause the paint to peel. A wide anchor chart will require more glue. You will have to work quickly to make sure the glue doesn't cool before you place and align the chart.

Hook and Loop Tape and Coins

Larger pieces of hook and loop tape and coins can be used to display your anchor charts. Select self-adhesive hook and loop pieces. The hook and loop tape will make it easy for your students to remove, use and replace the anchor chart. Be consistent about which side will be placed on the anchor charts and which will be adhered to the wall or surface area. For example, decide to stick all the loop (softer side) pieces to the charts. This makes it easier to exchange one chart for another.

Hook & Loop Coins are Perfect for Active Anchor Charts

Hooks

There are many brands of self-adhesive hooks. There are inexpensive hooks available at dollar stores, but the adhesive remains stuck on the wall when you remove the hook. The wall will be scratched or damaged if you use pressure to remove the adhesive.

I have tried many brands of hooks over the years. I have found 3M Command Hooks to be the safest and most reliable hooks on the market. They cost more than other brands, but they come in all kinds of shapes and colors. They are sturdy, easy to hang, super-easy to remove, and

leave no residue when removed. Your anchor charts will be made on a variety of materials. The thickest will probably be the foam board anchor charts. The thickness will not matter if you use the 3M hooks, because they have a wide selection of hooks.

Make sure to test a small piece of the adhesive on your display area.

Magnets

Magnets are great if you have a magnetic display surface. You'll want to make sure the magnets are strong enough to hold the weight of the anchor chart. Craft and hobby stores usually carry stronger magnets.

Paper Clips and Binder Clips

Thin display charts can easily be hung by paper clips. This may be the most inexpensive option, because most of us already have paper clips. If possible, use plastic coated paper clips. Metal paper clips have a tendency to rust or stain paper. Link several clips to increase the length of the chart.

Binder clips work nicely on thicker charts. You can also easily hang binder clips on hooks, because they have wider openings.

Push-pins

Push-pins will work if you will be in charge of moving the anchor charts. You may even decide your upper elementary students can handle the responsibility. Not all students can be trusted with these sharp pins. You'll need to keep the extras in your desk and keep track of the ones which are being used on your bulletin boards.

Putty or Wax Hangers

There are a few brands of putty and wax hangers which you can use to hang your anchor charts. Either will work nicely the first few times. They are easy to use and your students will be able to quickly move and re-attach their charts. However, tiny specs of dust and residue from the wall will collect in the putty and wax. Eventually, the dirt will cause putty and wax to lose tackiness. You can find putty or wax hangers online and in your teacher supply stores.

Staples

Staples are great for the anchor charts you will display on your bulletin boards. They are safer than the push pins, but they will leave tiny little holes in your charts. Those little holes will eventually expand and you will have to use paper reinforcements to repair the chart. Your principal will probably frown on the use of staples on your walls. The holes are tiny, but repeated use will leave the wall looking like it has termite tunnels.

Tape

The adhesive on painter's tape is safe on most surfaces. It leaves very little residue and is easy to move. It's a great tool for little hands which are trying to maneuver and display a chart. However, the tape will not remain tacky after it is moved a few times.

Duck tape is now available in various colors and patterns. You can use duck tape if you don't plan on moving the chart. However, this kind of tape tends to leave a sticky residue on the walls. It may even damage some of the wall paint once you remove it. Be sure to test it in a small and inconspicuous area before using it in a larger and more visible area.

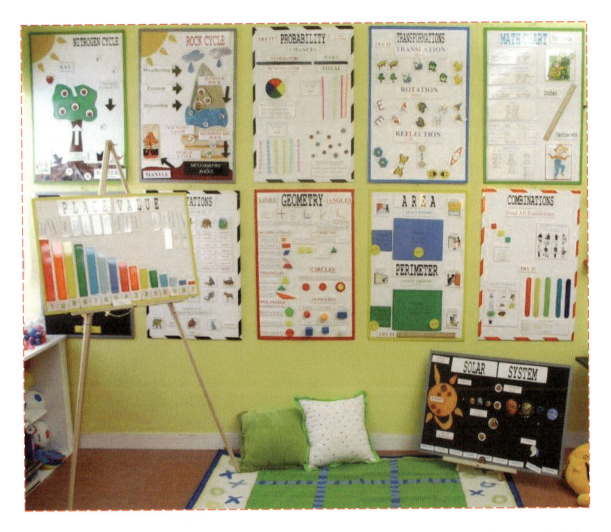

HOW TO USE YOUR *ACTIVE* ANCHOR CHARTS

- Add the Active Anchor Charts to your lesson plan. Have the Active Anchor Charts front and center as you deliver new lessons, review key terms and ideas, and review for quizzes and tests. Hang the chart up on a wall, prop it on a whiteboard, or place it on an easel as you introduce the lesson. You can work with a blank chart and add the information and materials as you cover the information. You may want to assign students the task of placing the titles and materials on the chart.

- Place the Active Anchor Charts in strategic places around the room. For example, by the classroom door where students wait for lunch, P.E., or other class changes. Place a few by your desk or whiteboard. Reach for them to add some spontaneity to a lesson, ease the stress of complex or tedious instruction, or to transition into another subject.

- Hang the Active Anchor Charts at an easy-to-reach level. Students can use them whenever there is a little time available. This could be in the morning before lessons begin, when they finish an assignment before others, during a subject or class transition, or while waiting on you or other teachers and students.

- If you use stations as a part of your instructional approach, then each Active Anchor Chart can be used as a stand-alone station. Simply add the Active Anchor Chart as a new station to the rotation system you are already using.

- Integrate the Active Anchor Charts into an existing station. For example, if you already have a station which focuses on place value, then add the Place Value Active Anchor Chart to the activities for that station.

- Prepare or have your students create small versions of Active Anchor Charts. If students are struggling with a particular learning objective, then they can take them home as homework or additional practice.

- Add the Active Anchor Charts to your game/reading/study corner. Students will begin to play with the activities on the charts and begin to see them as much more than a lesson.

Using Your *Active* Anchor Charts

Direct Teaching	Partner/ Group Work	Independent Work

Stations	Reading/ Study Corner	Tutoring/ Intervention	Homework

Using Multiple Contexts to Move Between L.O.T. & H.O.T.

Your active anchor charts are instant teaching tools that will help your students learn basic facts, ideas, and processes. A basic understanding of information is what we refer to as lower order thinking or L.O.T.

L.O.T. is fundamental. Within Bloom's Taxonomy students engaged in L.O.T. are working at the remember, understand, and application levels. All are critical in the learning process. Students use these basics to make the connections that will expand their understanding and help them reach higher order thinking or H.O.T.

You may have heard other terms used for H.O.T. It's often referred to as cognition, cognitive complexity, critical thinking, reasoning, rigor, depth of knowledge, deep thinking, and extended thinking. Within Bloom's Taxonomy students engaged in H.O.T. are working at the analysis, evaluation, and creation levels.

One of the keys to helping your students move *between* L.O.T. and H.O.T. is to change the context of the facts, ideas, or processes you are teaching. Note the use of the word *between*. This is intentional. *Between* represents the idea that each level of thinking is critical to the learning process. This means lower order thinking is as important as higher order thinking. It also indicates thinking is a fluid process where students continuously move between lower and higher order levels.

A unique context provides an opportunity to think critically about the characteristics of an element, how it fits into a different setting, how it can be adapted, how it connects with other ideas, or what other problems it can solve.

When students are able to apply a concept in a different context they are able to **analyze** the impact of the new context, **evaluate** the data between the various contexts, form new perspectives, and **create** solutions.

The learning experience becomes one where students are making kid-world, real-world, connections that are relevant and interesting to them. These connections increase motivation and students participate more. They also become more mindful of their time and their progress. They begin to see the value of the content and the learning process. An added bonus is that they stay on task and classroom discipline improves.

All of this is possible with one context. Let's think bigger... imagine the power that 2, 3, 4, 5, and more contexts will have on a student's ability to move between L.O.T. and H.O.T.

The point... *CONTEXT is KEY*.

CONTEXTS STARS

Use Contexts Stars with your active anchor charts to help your students move between L.O.T. and H.O.T.

A Context Star is a tool to plan and track the different contexts you are using with a concept. Aim to help your students use a concept in 5 or more contexts. The 5 contexts are not introduced all at once, but are instead considered over the course of a unit, reporting period, semester, or year.

3-CONTEXTS STAR

One way to use the 3-Contexts Star is for you to introduce the first context (remember one context is automatic as it is the one you use when you first teach a concept), guide your students through Context 2, and have students generate Context 3. The learning is reinforced with practice, a project, and/or review. Finally, an assessment, formative or summative, will allow you to pose lower and higher order questions to determine whether the learning objectives were met.

3-CONTEXTS STAR

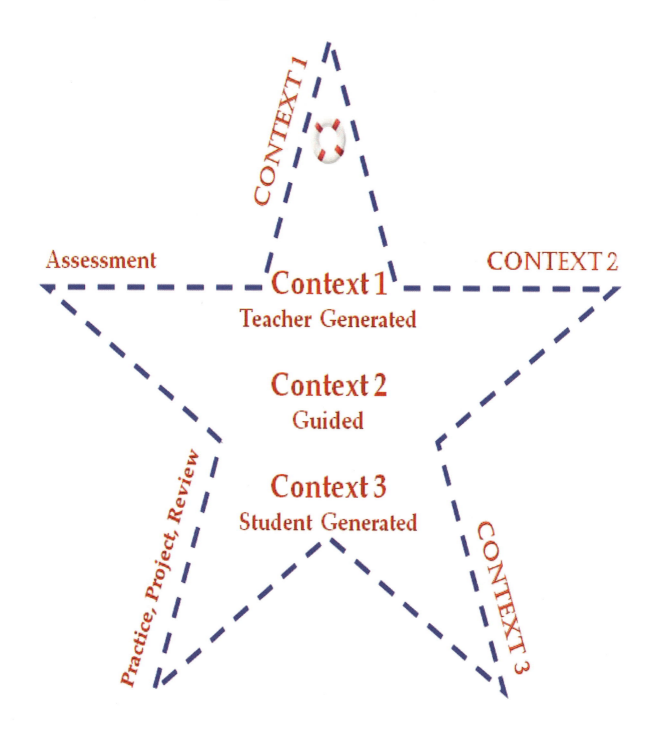

CONTEXT 1

Assessment

CONTEXT 2

Context 1
Teacher Generated

Context 2
Guided

Context 3
Student Generated

Practice, Project, Review

CONTEXT 3

5-CONTEXTS STAR

One way to use the 5-Contexts Star is for you to introduce 3 unique contexts (remember one context is automatic as it is the one you use when you first teach a concept). Your students use your 3 contexts to generate 2 unique contexts on their own.

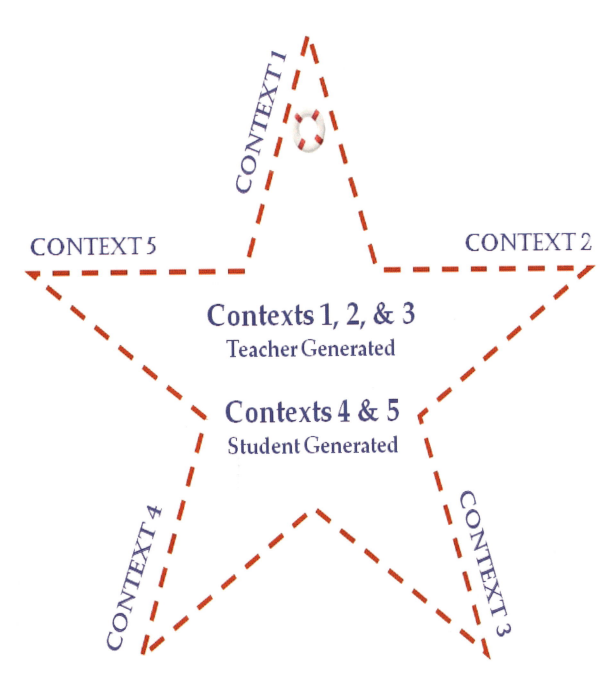

CONTEXT 5   CONTEXT 2

Contexts 1, 2, & 3
Teacher Generated

Contexts 4 & 5
Student Generated

CONTEXT 1

CONTEXT 4

CONTEXT 3

CONTEXTS STARS AND ACTIVE ANCHOR CHARTS

Your active anchor chart already presents information in ONE context. This is the same context you will likely use when you are direct teaching.

You can easily use your active anchor chart and the Contexts Stars to move between L.O.T. and H.O.T.

Attach a CONTEXTS STAR to the Active Anchor Chart. Use it to track different contexts that are related to the content presented on the chart.

Add visuals and manipulatives to represent multiple contexts on the active anchor chart. You don't have to display all of these at once. Keep them and other materials in a plastic bag or large envelope. Use hook and loop tape, double sided tape, or glue to attach the bag or envelope to the board.

Refer to other contexts as you are teaching. Apply the facts, ideas, and processes to various contexts. Work through thinking levels as you demonstrate how to evaluate, analyze, and create. Remember, the contexts are not introduced all at once. Instead, you work through them over time.

Teach your students about the CONTEXTS STARS. Consider giving them copies of the stars or have them draw the star in a journal. They can fill the contexts in as they work with the active anchor charts.

Here are two snapshots of the CONTEXTS STARS. Larger versions are provided on the next two pages.

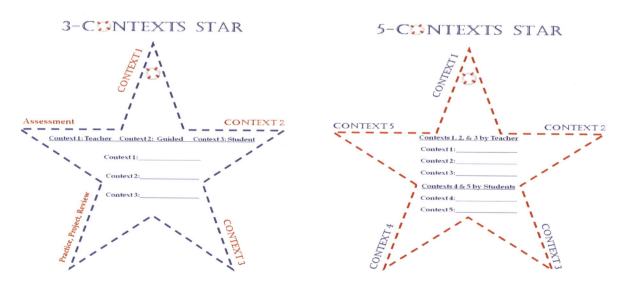

3-CONTEXTS STAR

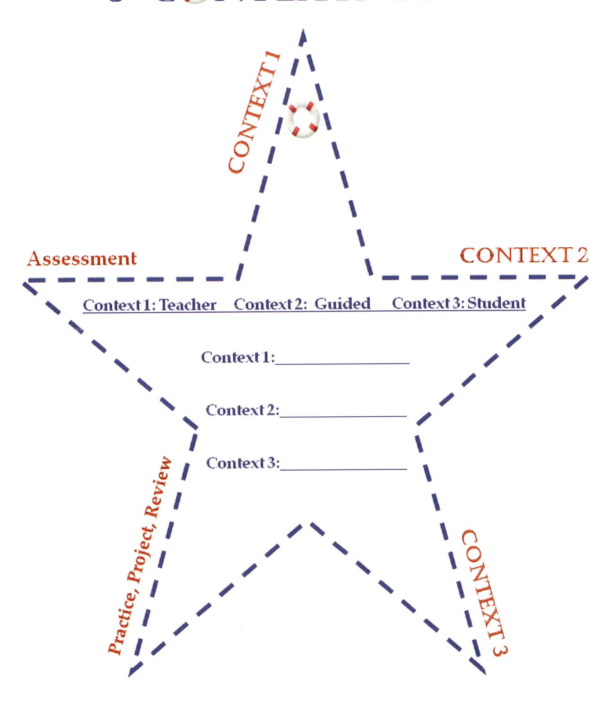

CONTEXT 1

Assessment

CONTEXT 2

Context 1: Teacher   Context 2: Guided   Context 3: Student

Context 1: _____

Context 2: _____

Context 3: _____

Practice, Project, Review

CONTEXT 3

5-CONTEXTS STAR

CONTEXT 1

CONTEXT 5

CONTEXT 2

Contexts 1, 2, & 3 by Teacher

Context 1:_____

Context 2:_____

Context 3:_____

Contexts 4 & 5 by Students

Context 4:_____

Context 5:_____

CONTEXT 4

CONTEXT 3

Information about Bloom's Taxonomy can be found in the works of:

Anderson, L. W., & Krathwohl, D. R. (Eds.). (2001)

Bloom, B. S. & Krathwohl, D. R. (1956)

Rotating Your *Active* Anchor Charts

Once you have a collection of Active Anchor Charts, you'll find it challenging to keep them all on display.

Your classroom walls are prime real estate, and you will need to rotate the charts on a regular basis.

Consider only displaying the charts which relate to the unit you are currently covering. In some cases, you will want to keep a few charts on display throughout the school year.

Ask yourself the following questions:

- Which concepts continue to present a struggle for your students?

- Which Active Anchor Charts continue to be a hit with your students? They may turn to these charts, because they have become fun games or challenges. You'll want to keep these charts handy, because they are constructive uses of spare time.

Classroom Walls

are

Prime Real Estate

Consider which

charts cover...

1. **Difficult concepts**

2. **Activities kids love**

3. **Information and facts needed throughout the year**

- Which Active Anchor Charts serve as references, because they are important reminders for a majority of concepts? They might present strategies, processes, or fundamental facts. These could be story elements, types of graphs, the writing process, problem solving strategies, or multiplication facts.

ACTIVE ANCHOR CHART BEST PRACTICES

- Create Active Anchor Charts which are aligned to the learning objectives and be sure to include the objective on the board.

- Use only one concept or learning objective per board.

- Use color. Don't use words when a visual will do.

- Engage as many senses as possible: Sight, Sound, Touch, and Smell.

- Use 3-dimensional objects and moveable pieces.

- Display the Active Anchor Charts and keep them in the same spot during the school year – students will automatically check that spot when they have a question.

- Include the anchor charts in your lesson plans – make them a part of your weekly routine. Use them in small or whole group direct teaching, group work, partnered work, one-to-one instruction, and independent practice. Include them as a part of the main lesson, in reviews, and during tutoring.

- Refer to the anchor charts often and encourage your students to do the same.

- Teach students to remove the charts from the wall and use them when there is time.

- Have students write notes after they have used the anchor charts. Their notes could include key words, key ideas, questions, comments, or a sketch of the board.

- Leave the charts up during quizzes and weekly tests, but take them down for benchmarks (let your students know the charts will be taken down).

- Give students time to review the anchor charts before a quiz or test.

- Take a picture of your anchor chart. Create a word document with the picture or print out the picture. Add notes to the image – write what items need clarification, what additional materials would be useful, what to remove, and what worked and what didn't. Keep all the documents in a folder (digital or a real folder) and make adjustments as necessary – eventually they'll be perfect!

REFERENCES

Anderson, L. W., & Krathwohl, D. R. (Eds.). (2001). A taxonomy for learning, teaching and assessing: A revision of Bloom's taxonomy of educational objectives. New York : Longman.

Bloom, B. S. & Krathwohl, D. R. (1956). Taxonomy of educational objectives: The classification of educational goals, by a committee of college and university examiners. New York , Longmans.

Buzan, T. & Buzan, B. (1996). *The mind map book*. New York: Plume.

Hockley, W. (2008). The picture superiority effect in associative recognition. *Memory and Cognition, (36)*7, 1351 – 1359.

Marzano, R. J., Pickering, D. J., & Pollock, J. E. (2001). *Classroom instruction that works*. Alexandria, VA: Association for Supervision and Curriculum Development.

Thompson, V. A. & Paivio, A. (1994). Memory for pictures and sounds: Independence of auditory and visual codes. *Canadian Journal of Experimental Psychology, (48)*3, 380 – 398.

Thank You for Selecting

ACTIVE ANCHOR CHARTS
Taking Anchor Charts from "Read Me to Try Me"

Please let us know if you have any questions:
contactus@treetopsecret.com

Find additional resources & support on our
Tree Top Secret Website

http://treetopsecret.com/

Stay in Touch...

 https://www.facebook.com/treetopsecret

https://twitter.com/treetopsecret

 http://www.pinterest.com/treetopsecret/

Made in the USA
Lexington, KY
20 August 2015